50 TIPS
TO GET YOU
ORGANIZED
In Ten Minutes or Less!

Bonnie Joy Dewkett, CPO®
Paris Love

Published by The Joyful Organizer® and Organize With Love
P.O. Box 585
Ridgefield, Connecticut 06877

10 9 8 7 6 5 4 3 2 1

ISBN 9781451592511

Printed in The United States of America
Set in Helvetica Neue, Rockwell, Engravers MT, Goudy Old Style
Book Design by Matt Dewkett

Disclaimer:

Every effort has been made to make this book as complete and accurate
as possible, but no warranty or fitness is implied. The information is pro-
vided is on an "as is" basis. The author and the publisher shall have nei-
ther liability nor responsibility to any person or entity with respect to any
loss or damages arising from the information contained in this book.

Any mention of a brand name product or company should not be consid-
ered an endorsement of that product or company. The author has no
affiliation with any manufacturer or company and is not paid to endorse
any products.

Dedication

We would like to thank our families for their continuing support.

Bonnie Joy Dewkett, CPO®

Bonnie Joy Dewkett, CPO® is a nationally recognized organizing expert, author, motivational speaker, and internet radio personality. She began organizing as a child when she would organize her toys, and she has been organizing ever since. After helping numerous friends and family members organize their homes, she decided to make it a full time career in 2006.

She has gained a nationwide audience through her radio show, The Joy of Organizing, which has become an instant success on the Diva Toolbox Radio Network. Airing weekly, the show provides practical organizing tips and tricks for busy families. In addition to her own advice, she has interviewed many of the country's top organizing experts, including Julie Morgenstern, Barbara Hemphill, Barry Izsak, and Diane Albright.

Bonnie's expert advice has been featured in NAPO News, locally in many newspapers throughout the New York City Metro area, and nationally in *Better Homes and Gardens Secrets of Getting Organized* annual edition.

Bonnie has achieved the prestigious designation of Certified Professional Organizer, CPO®, from The Board of Certification for Professional Organizers. Making her one of only six in the State of Connecticut, and less than twenty-five in all of New England. She is also proud to be a member of The National Association of Professional Organizers (NAPO).

Bonnie received a B.S. in Resource and Agribusiness Management from The University of Maine in 2001. She is currently completing work on her M.B.A. from Nichols College, which she expects to complete in the Spring of 2011.

Paris Love

Paris Love, President of Organize With Love a full service consulting and organizing firm. We incorporate project management, organizing, and consulting into our area of expertise. We teach our clients how to prioritize, execute and maximize their time by using a variety of procedures and methods. Our methods are based on observations and interaction among individuals within the workplace.

Paris has written articles for NAPO News, Baldwin Parent, Brown-Skin Magazine, OnlineOrganizing and Home Based Quarterly Magazine. Paris have been featured in numerous publications as well as being an expert writer for Ezine Articles. Paris has been interviewed and featured on several Radio and Television shows and has been the Organizing Expert for IKEA-Atlanta.

An active member of the National Association of Professional Organizers (NAPO). Paris has served on the NAPO-GA Executive Board and Board of Directors and has held the positions of Librarian and Secretary. She currently holds the Historian and Ambassador positions within the Georgia Chapter. Paris is a member of NAPO's Golden Circle, a prestigious designation denotes an elevated level of experience within the professional organizing industry. Golden Circle members possess at least five years of proven professional organizing work activity.

Paris holds a Masters degree in Human Resource Management and a Masters in Business Administration. She also holds undergraduate degrees in Psychology and Fashion Design. Paris is currently working on her Ph.D. in Industrial Organizational Psychology.

Table of Contents

The book is set up to give you an example of common organizing challenges in each area of the home.

Foreword   **1**

Chapter One: The Living Room   **3**
The living room is often a focal point in your home, it is where you relax in the evening, and can often be where you entertain guests. Clearing clutter from your living room will allow you to invite friends over again, without the stress!

Chapter Two: The Bedroom   **10**
The bedroom should be your sanctuary, is it? Clearing clutter out of your bedroom will help you relax after a hard day at work, sleep better, and get ready faster the next morning.

Chapter Three: The Kitchen   **16**
The kitchen is the heart of the home. It is where you fuel your family to take on each new day. How can you cook when you have more clutter than food?

Chapter Four: The Office   **22**
The office is the financial center of the home. Clutter can make an office inefficient, and who wants to spend more time than they have to paying bills?

Chapter Five: Throughout Your Home   **28**
Ready, Set, Go! Some more quick tips that you can implement today to make a difference in your home!

Foreword

We are passionate about helping you live an organized and clutter-free life. Each **Love Challenge** only requires a few minutes of your time to implement a **Joyful Solution.**

So many of our clients are always telling us they are waiting to get organized until they have more time, more money, or more space. The truth is, those things may never happen, so what are you waiting for?

Live the best life you can, **today!**

Introduction

When we ask our clients the number one reason for not getting organized the answer is: **TIME.** This book is designed to help you get organized, and get rid of the clutter, ten minutes at a time. Everyone can find ten minutes a day to help themselves, and their family, live a calmer, more organized life.

While these tasks are designed to take **ten minutes or less,** some will require planning and purchasing organizational tools. If you cannot complete a task today, make an appointment with yourself on your calendar to complete it at a later date. Put items to purchase on your shopping list immediately.

Don't get bogged down in the details, keep moving, and make decisions quickly.

Ready? Set? Get organizing!

Good luck!
Bonnie and Paris

CHAPTER ONE:
THE LIVING ROOM

Love Challenge #1 - Are there magazines and catalogs that you haven't read?

Joyful Solution: Make a list of all of your subscriptions. If you don't read it anymore, call to cancel. (They will give you a refund, or you can change the address on your subscription to a local school, senior center, or library.)

If you never purchase anything from a company's catalog, call and request to be removed from their mailing list.

Love Challenge #2 - Are you tired of your living room furniture?

Joyful Solution: If you are unhappy with your furniture, obtain a quote to reupholster. Or, visit a local furniture super store, such as Ikea, for inexpensive options to replace pieces.

Also, consider using slipcovers to change the look of the room quickly and cost effectively. You may consider adding throw pillows or new curtains to add a little flair for not a lot of cost.

Love Challenge #3 - Has your living room become the "catch-all" area for bills?

Joyful Solution: Gather all of the bills and bring them to the location where you would sit and pay them.

Love Challenge #4 - Need more storage?

Joyful Solution: If you don't have a lot of storage in your living room, use short totes for the space under your couch to house items, buy a storage ottoman, or install shelving. If you want to make any of these changes, take measurements today and look at some options online. (Time yourself so you don't spend more than 10 minutes browsing.)

Love Challenge #5 - Do you or anyone in your family have clothes or shoes lying around this area?

Joyful Solution: Remove all clothing from the living room, and move it to the laundry area. Use a laundry basket to gather items that don't belong in the living room. This is a great task for a child! Then return the items to each family member's closet. Make everyone responsible for his or her own items.

Love Challenge #6 - Do you have a brown thumb?

Joyful Solution: If the plants are dead, throw them away. If they are not quite there, donate them to a neighbor or senior center.

Love Challenge #7 - Do you have many photos waiting for a home?

Joyful Solution: If you have empty photo albums start by putting one picture in from your boxes of photos every night. Before you know it, you will have a working album. If you have no intention of using them, sell the albums on EBay or Craig's List.

Love Challenge #8 -When was the last time you dusted the television?

Joyful Solution: Mount your TV on the wall for extra storage space, and so it will collect less dust. Buy a TV mounting kit and recruit a friend. You will need a drill and to locate a stud in your wall. A representative at a technology store will assist you in obtaining the correct mount for your TV.

Take a photo of the back of your TV before you visit the store to make this process easier.

Love Challenge #9 - Are you baffled by a certain odor in your home?

Joyful Solution: Use candles, oil based air fresheners, or open windows to keep the air fresh in your living space. Also consider using a HEPA filter to filter out air impurities. Turn the filter on or light the candles for the 10 minutes you are organizing to create a more spa-like atmosphere.

Love Challenge #10 - Is your coat closet cluttered?

Joyful Solution: Store coats in an entry way closet, or hall storage bin. Get rid of any coats you don't wear. Install an extra shelf above and below the closet rod in your hall closet for extra storage.

Place baskets (one for each family member) on these shelves to house gloves, scarves and even small shoes and sports equipment. Leave extra hangers in this closet for guests' coasts.

Love Challenge #11 – Do you still have unpacked boxes from a long ago move?

Joyful Solution: If you don't remember what is in the boxes, you don't need them. Take a quick peek (don't remove anything from the box unless you intend to keep it and find it a home immediately.) Call to have the boxes picked up by your local donation center.

Love Challenge #12 - Are there water stains on the coffee table or other furniture?

Joyful Solution: Have a piece of glass custom cut for your coffee table (usually this costs under $50) to avoid stains and make the top of your coffee table easily cleaned.

During today's 10 minutes, call for a quote on this glass or to have the piece refinished.

CHAPTER TWO: THE BEDROOM

Love Challenge #13 – Pile of books by the bed?

Joyful Solution: Keep books in your office or living area. However, if you cannot, confine them to a bookshelf in your bedroom. Donate read books regularly. Limit yourself to two books by the bedside stand and one or two magazines. If you have a drawer, keep them in there.

Love Challenge #14 - Do you have a designated area for laundry?

Joyful Solution: Have a spot in your bedroom to put all dirty laundry. If you have space, separate darks, delicate and lights in separate baskets. Also, use a basket for "semi dirty" items that can be worn again.

Love Challenge #15 - Is there any broken furniture in the bedroom?

Joyful Solution: Have broken furniture repaired or replace it. Visit your local hardware store for furniture glue, paint touch up, etc. Call for a quote to fix broken furniture now.

Love Challenge #16 - Is there any food in the bedroom?

Joyful Solution: Remove dirty dishes every morning or at night. Start with removing them all right now.

Love Challenge #17 - Do you have burned out or missing light bulbs?

Joyful Solution: Replace missing light bulbs as soon as they burn out. Keep some extras located on each floor.

Love Challenge #18 - Are there any stains on the floor or carpet?

Joyful Solution: Call for a carpet cleaning today. Or, rent a carpet cleaner on your next trip to the supermarket. They are inexpensive and even kids can help with the cleaning process.

Love Challenge #19 - Does your child leave their artwork on the walls?

Joyful Solution: Use Magic Erasers to clean walls. Do one room a day until you have done the whole house.

Love Challenge #20 - Is there money lying around without a designated home?

Joyful Solution: Set one place in your bedroom to store change and another for paper bills. Make a point to "cash it in" every month or so. Kids love helping with this! Use the money you get back to buy a family surprise, fund trips to the movies, or even save for a vacation.

Some banks offer change exchange services for free.

Love Challenge #21 - Do you have multiple knick-knacks?

Joyful Solution: Limit the number of knick-knacks you have on your dresser, etc. Install shelving and display boxes to hold excess.

Love Challenge #22 - When was the last time you dusted the blinds? Are they old, broken or dirty?

Joyful Solution: Visit various blind stores to view low cost options for blinds, curtains etc. Even super stores now have a vast array of window treatments. To save even more money, buy energy efficient treatments. They can pay for themselves in the energy they save!

Keep in mind everything you install should be easy to clean, preferably machine washable.

Keep a step stool on every floor so you can quickly access hard to reach areas.

Love Challenge #23 - Are you utilizing your bedroom as an office?

Joyful Solution: Try to keep office items out of your bedroom. However, if you must store them in your bedroom, do so in an area you can close and then have out of sight. Remove office items now or purchased a closable desk to house office items. Or, considering converting a small closet into an office area.

Love Challenge #24 - Is the cat's litter box in your bedroom?

Joyful Solution: Keep pet litter boxes out of your bedroom at all costs. Find a new home for it now. To make cleanup easier, but a small plastic or rubber mat to fit underneath the litter box. This can be shaken out and wiped down must easier than a carpet or floor.

Love Challenge #25 - Do you have a television in your bedroom?

Joyful Solution: If possible, keep television in a piece of furniture that you can close and then have out of sight.

For better use of space, mount your TV on the wall if possible.

CHAPTER THREE: THE KITCHEN

Love Challenge #26 - Do you have mail piled on your counters?

Joyful Solution: Place all mail in an in-bin. Sort this bin out daily or every other day.

Love Challenge #27 - Are there dishes in the sink?

Joyful Solution: Load and unload the dishwasher daily. (Kids can do this at a young age as long as they can reach the cabinets to put the dishes away.)

Love Challenge #28 - Are your cabinets cluttered?

Joyful Solution: For two weeks mark with a piece of blue painters tape everything you use in your kitchen. If you don't use it or love it, donate it.

Love Challenge #29 - Do you have any broken dishes?

Joyful Solution: Throw away broken dishes. Buy an extra set when you purchase dishes so you can replace out broken plates easily. Or go online now to find replacement dishes. Check out http://www.replacements.com/

Love Challenge #30 – Huge pile of papers and not sure how to deal with it?

Joyful Solution: Flip the pile over and start from the bottom. Most of those papers are too old to be useful.

Love Challenge #31 - Are you saving plastic bags for a rainy day?

Joyful Solution: Use reusable bags when possible. Keep a maximum of five to ten disposable plastic bags on hand. Recycle the others or use them for pet waste, or car garbage bags. There will always be more plastic bags coming in. Throw the ones you have away and start from zero. Give yourself a limit on the amount you store.

Love Challenge #32 - Do you save the condiments packages from restaurants?

Joyful Solution: Throw away any fast food condiment packages. Otherwise take the time to refill larger condiment containers.

Love Challenge #33 - Is your pantry cluttered?

Joyful Solution: Although a complete pantry organization will take more than ten minutes you can break it up unto smaller tasks.

Throw away five expired items.

Donate five items your family doesn't eat.

Make a list of items you need to buy.

Make a list of what you have and store it in the closet itself. Even if you can visually see everything in the closet, you will know what you have.

Love Challenge #34 - When was the last time you cleaned the stovetop?

Joyful Solution: Clean your store top weekly. Otherwise you are in danger of having a grease fire.

Love Challenge #35 - Do you have multiple junk drawers?

Joyful Solution: It is okay to have one junk drawer. However, junk drawers are normally catch alls for stuff you just aren't ready to throw away yet. Be merciless in what you keep and need in this space. Today your task is to throw away at least 10 things in the junk drawer.

Love Challenge #36 - When was the last time you cleaned the fridge?

Joyful Solution: Clean out the fridge once a week for expired food, leftovers, etc. Make it the same day every week, preferably right before you grocery shop. Today's task is to wipe down the inside of the door, the shelves and throw out any expired or moldy food.

Tomorrow's task is to do the same with the freezer.

Love Challenge #37 – Are there any missing piece to your cookware set?

Joyful Solution: Make sure you have the lids to all of your pots and pans by matching them all up. If you need more small pans, buy these and get rid of some larger ones you already own.

Having a whole set is not important, the important thing is to match up your needs with what you own.

CHAPTER FOUR:
THE OFFICE

Love Challenge #38 - Are you trying to tame the paper monster?

Joyful Solution: Purchase papersorting bins and give each a title. For example, mail to read, bills to pay, wishlist, etc. No paper should be thrown onto the desk without first being assigned a category. Touch each paper only once. At that time, put it in your action (to do) pile, file it or throw it away.

Love Challenge #39 - Is your computer monitor dusty?

Joyful Solution: Make sure to clean your computer screen and keyboard weekly. Keep supplies to do so close to your workstation.

Love Challenge #40 – Are your cords an eye sore?

Joyful Solution: Use cord management systems (available any many organization stores) to label and manage cords. This will eliminate frustration when you need to find a cord. You can also use multi-colored electrical tape to label cords.

Love Challenge #41 - Are you saving empty ink cartridges?

Joyful Solution: Recycle empty ink cartridges. Drop them off at your local office store, or use a program such as Cartridges for Kids to obtain a credit for your local school.

HP will even send you a prepaid envelope to return empty cartridges.

Love Challenge #42 - Do you have a clock in your office?

Joyful Solution: Install an inexpensive clock on the wall above your workspace so you can keep track of time.

Love Challenge #43 - Not sure what to file?

Joyful Solution: Call your attorney and accountant and ask what documents you need to keep for tax purposes and ask how long you need to keep them for. Everything else is at your discretion. Remember, we only ever touch 20% of what we file ever again.

Love Challenge #44 - Has your office become the catchall area?

Joyful Solution: Have everyone in your family come into the office and claim his or her personal items. Items left after this will be donated or discarded.

Love Challenge #45 - Are you utilizing the equipment in your office?

Joyful Solution: Any unused computer equipment should be donated after any personal information is erased. Use Craig's List or Free Cycle to get rid of items quickly and for free.

Love Challenge #46 - Are you missing a desk?

Joyful Solution: If you do not have a desk in your office, obtain a workspace as soon as possible. You can purchase a table from a flea market or a desk from a super store or you can use two small filing cabinets and a large board across the top. You can even use a portable kitchen island cart as a portable office.

Love Challenge #47 - Do you hate your chair?

Joyful Solution: Make sure your work chair is comfortable. If you don't want to purchase another chair, use pillows or back supports to make the one you have more comfortable. Consider using a fitness ball or barstool instead of a traditional chair.

Love Challenge #48 - Are you losing files?

Joyful Solution: Keep all papers in one location. This doesn't have to be in the living space. Consider storing files in the basement or a small closet somewhere. Just make sure you can get to the space to file papers when necessary.

Love Challenge #49 - Do you have an unrealistic to-do list?

Joyful Solution: Create more than one to do list for yourself. Use one list for today, one for the week, one for the month and one for long term. Crossing items off will make you feel accomplished and give you momentum. If your list is currently overwhelming and messy, rewrite it. When doing so, take off a few items are not good uses of your time.

Love Challenge #50 - Is your trash can overflowing?

Joyful Solution: Empty your office trashcan and shredder once a week. Leave a little space in your kitchen trash and combine them when taking them out.

CHAPTER FIVE: THROUGHOUT YOUR HOME

More things you can do in **Ten Minutes or Less!**

Start Your Timer, Ready...Set...GO!!!

✓Empty trash

✓Shred mail

✓Return a call
(Tell the person you are calling, "I have five minutes but I really wanted to talk to you about...)

✓Empty recycling containers

✓Delete five emails

✓Help kids clean out their school bag

✓Vacuum

✓Fold blankets/throws in living / family room

✓Put CDs and DVDs back in their cases

✓Water plants or remove dead plants

✓Call to be taken off one mailing list

✓Wipe down outside of fridge

Thank you again for purchasing our book! We hope that it inspires you to tackle the organizing projects you have putting off.

Feel free to visit our websites for more organizing tips.

http://www.organizewithlove.com
http://www.thejoyfulorganizer.com

Wishing you much success in your organizing endeavors,

Paris and Bonnie